Pat's Cats

by Liza Charlesworth • illustrated by Kelly Kennedy

SCHOLASTIC INC.

New York • Toronto • London • Auckland • Sydney
Mexico City • New Delhi • Hong Kong • Buenos Aires

Designed by Grafica, Inc.
ISBN: 978-0-545-68619-8
Copyright © 2009 by Lefty's Editorial Services.
All rights reserved. Published by Scholastic Inc.
SCHOLASTIC, LET'S LEARN READERS™, and associated logos are trademarks and/or registered trademarks of Scholastic Inc.

12 11 10 9 8 7 6 5 4 3 2 1   14 15 16 17 18 19/0

Printed in China.

The At Family

What Is a Word Family?
A word family is a group of words that rhyme and share the same spelling pattern, such as *Pat, cat,* and *hat.* Read this story to learn more *-at* words!

Meet **Pat**.
Pat is a member of the **At** family.

Now it is time to meet **Pat**'s **cat**s.

This **cat** is very **fat**!

That cat is very **flat**!

This **cat** sleeps on a **mat**!

That cat wears a fancy **hat**!

This **cat** hangs out with a **bat**!

That cat is pals with a **gnat**!

This **cat** is a bit of a **brat**!

That cat likes to **chat** and **chat**!

What is the same
about every **cat**?

They all love **Pat**
and **that** is **that**!

Word Family House

Point to the *-at* word in each room and read it aloud.

bat	fat	mat
cat	gnat	rat
sat	Pat	hat
chat		flat
that		brat

Word Family Riddles

Read each *-at* riddle. Then point to the answer in the word box.

1 I say "Meow."

2 I am a flying mammal.

3 I am a little rug.

4 I am a tiny insect.

5 You wear me on your head.

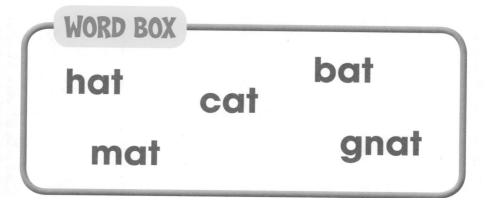

WORD BOX

hat

cat

bat

mat

gnat

Word Family Bingo

Which words belong to the *-at* family? Cover them with buttons or pennies. Get four in a row to win!

sock	play	cat	fan
gnat	hat	bat	jay
that	rake	chat	rat
mop	rock	mat	flat

Answer: Bingo is the third column down: cat, bat, chat, mat.